To-Do Lists of the Dead

To-Do Lists of the Dead

JONATHAN KATZ

**Andrews McMeel
Publishing**

Kansas City

00 01 02 03 04 BIN 10 9 8 7 6 5 4 3 2

ISBN: 0-7407-0035-9

Library of Congress Cataloging-in-Publication Data

Katz, Jonathan.
  To-do lists of the dead / Jonathan Katz.
     p. cm.
  ISBN 0-7407-0035-9 (pbk.)
   1. American wit and humor. I. Title.

PN6162 .K38 2000
818'.5402–dc21

                  99-057121

ATTENTION: SCHOOLS AND BUSINESSES

Andrews McMeel books are available at quantity discounts with bulk purchase for
educational, business, or sales promotional use. For information, please write to:
Special Sales Department, Andrews McMeel Publishing, 4520 Main Street, Kansas
City, Missouri 64111.

Contents

DEDICATED TO AND INSPIRED BY
ALL THE PEOPLE IN THE BOOK WHO
LEAD SUCH COLORFUL LIVES,
WITH THE POSSIBLE EXCEPTION
OF SONNY BONO.

thanks to my wife Suzan
Bonnie Burns
Mary Catherine Tucker
Colleen Mohyde
Julie Roberts
Jen Sneider
Melissa Bardin Galsky
David Gelles
John Kasiewikz
David Mamet

and a special thanks to Bill Braudis for his help
with this project and for
providing additional material.

Introduction

To-Do Lists of the Dead used to be an idea for a book, but then I told it to so many people that I thought it would be more efficient to just write it down. I guess it grew out of two areas of my life: my desire to make people laugh and my longing for organization. I'm talking about the capacity to organize my day, my week, or even my life. I used to spend hours alphabetizing and cross-referencing my jokes and moving all my long-sleeve shirts to one side of my closet and my short-sleeve shirts to the other. I know it doesn't sound like fun, but think about it for a minute. Okay, it still doesn't sound like fun, but neither is looking for shirts . . . or jokes.

To-Do Lists of the Dead

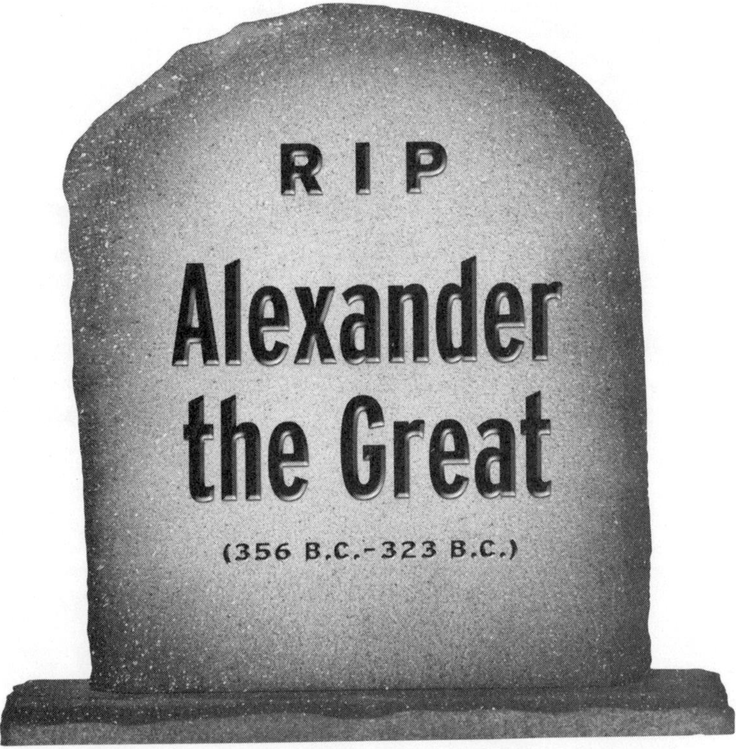

RIP
Alexander the Great
(356 B.C.-323 B.C.)

ALEXANDER

✓ 1. Conquer Persian empire.

2. Push my "world brotherhood of all men" theory but take time to smell the roses.

3. Tell the Greeks to worship me as a god but try to keep a straight face.

Don't let the name go to my head, and don't let on that it was my idea.

RIP

Marie Antoinette

(NOV. 2, 1755–OCT. 16, 1793)

To-Do

✓1. Let them eat cake and/or gelato.

✓2. Tell Henry "the whatever" that he is a big, fat pig.

✓3. Get more necklaces.

✓4. Get a haircut. (Just a little off the top.)

RIP

P.T. Barnum

(JULY 5, 1810–APRIL 7, 1891)

TO-DO

✓ 1. Ask Ringling brothers if they want to go in on summer house.

2. Tell Bailey to stop calling me. (Circus my ass!)

✓ 3. Get a really sophisticated stopwatch.

✓ 4. Count the number of suckers born in a twenty-four-hour period to test thesis.

TO-DO

5. Look into idea of a low-budget freak show:

- bearded man
- mental midget
- Siamese cats
- not a fat lady but a woman who is premenstrual (just a little bloated)
- emotionally strong man

Or, instead of Siamese cats, we could have two guys with a joint checking account...

✓ 6. Lie down.

RIP

Alexander Graham Bell

(MARCH 3, 1847–AUG. 2, 1922)

To-Do List:

✓1. Deposit check.

✓2. Pick up dry cleaning.

✓3. Invent telephone.

4. Get unlisted number.

Alexander Graham Bell

To-Do List:

5. Don't let people take the
"I need you, Watson"
line out of context.
(I don't really need him.)

This telephone thing is gonna be big
but it will never replace the telegram!

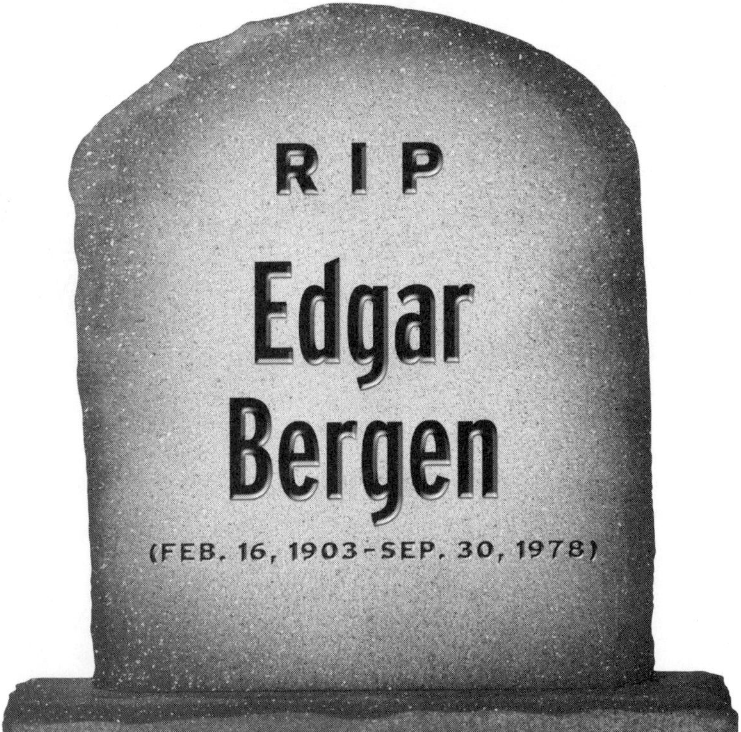
RIP
Edgar
Bergen
(FEB. 16, 1903-SEP. 30, 1978)

Things To-Do Today

✓ 1. Ventriloquism on radio? (Hey, if they're gonna pay me.)

2. Drop the puppet from the act.

✓ 3. Get picture hooks.

4. Get pictures.

5. Don't put words in other people's mouths.

Don't let Candice
go into the business...
she's too vulnerable.

RIP

Justice Harry
Blackmun

(NOV. 12, 1908–MARCH 4, 1999)

Justice Harry Blackmon
Supreme Court
United States of America

✓ 1. Find out which one is Wade
(but be discreet).

✓ 2. Buy condoms—the lady at the
end of the jury box is looking
hot!

3. Suggest to the others my idea
of yellow robes…could be fun.

Heads it's Roe;
Tails it's Wade.

RIP

Humphrey
Bogart

(DEC. 25, 1899-JAN. 14, 1957)

FROM THE DESK OF
HUMPHREY BOGART

✓ 1. *Learn ballroom dancing.*

2. *Get new agent.*

✓ 3. *Work on Oscar acceptance speech.*

4. *Get speech therapy.*

RIP

Sonny Bono

(FEB. 16, 1935–JAN. 5, 1998)

To-Do This Week

. . . .

Monday—

Tuesday—Try to reason with Cher and stop telling her she's nothing without me. (Not a bad name for a song, though . . .)

Wednesday—Maybe i could live with "Cher and Sonny."

Thursday—

Things To-Do This Week

Friday—How about "Cher, with special guest Sonny Bono," your fucking husband and the reason you're working today, babe!

Sat/Sun—

✓ Monday—Let this thing die a natural death.

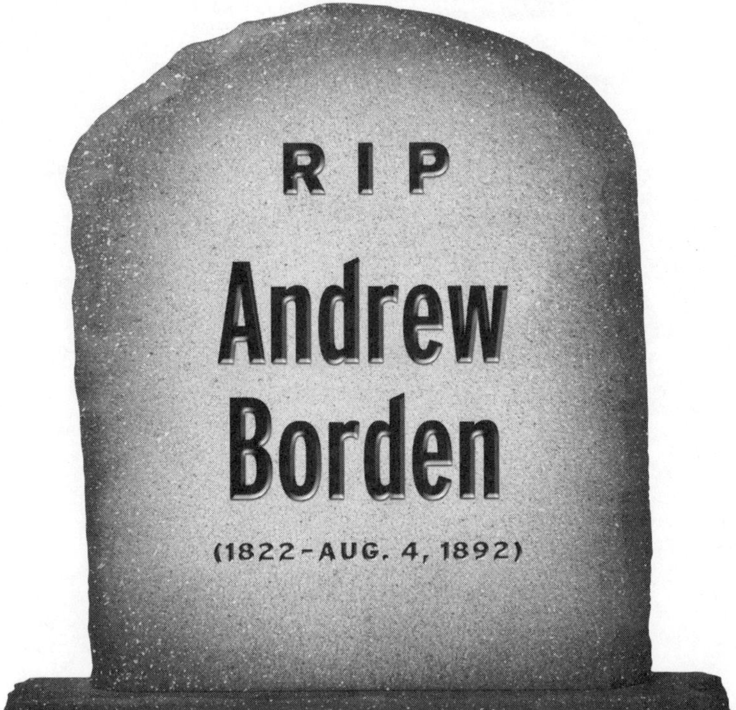

RIP
Andrew Borden
(1822–AUG. 4, 1892)

Things To-Do

✓ 1. Rethink curfew for Lizzie. (She seems a little cranky.)

2. Find my ax.

3. Lift curfew for Lizzie. After all she is thirty-two years old. But right now, find that ax!

RIP

Lizzie Borden

(JULY 19, 1860–JUNE 1, 1927)

To-Do List –

1. Try to control my temper.

2. Explain to parents that I am thirty-two years old and my own woman.

To-Do List –

✓ 3. The hell with it—hack my parents to death in a way that will someday make a great children's poem.

✓ 4. Burn blood-stained dress.

✓ 5. Bring freshly hacked flowers for the jury.

RIP

Louis Braille

(JAN. 4, 1809 – JAN. 6, 1852)

⠇⠕⠥⠊⠎ ⠃⠗⠁⠊⠇⠇⠑
Louis Braille
....

1. Figure out a good name for the system I've developed for reading.

2. Tell her parents I'm practicing "the system."

If this "Braille" thing catches on
I could give up the organ & the cello...
who am I kidding?

RIP

Buddha

(C. 563 B.C.–C. 483 B.C.)

To-Do

✓1. Become enlightened.

✓2. Become one with everything or, at the most, possibly two.

3. Find out if the crowds are followers or just people who can't get around me.

To-Do

We are what we think ... All that we are arises with our thoughts. To live a pure unselfish life, one must count nothing as one's own in the midst of abundance ... you are what you eat ... An insincere and evil friend is more to be feared than a wild beast (this is too easy)....

you don't know what you've got till it's gone... love means never having to say you're sorry...

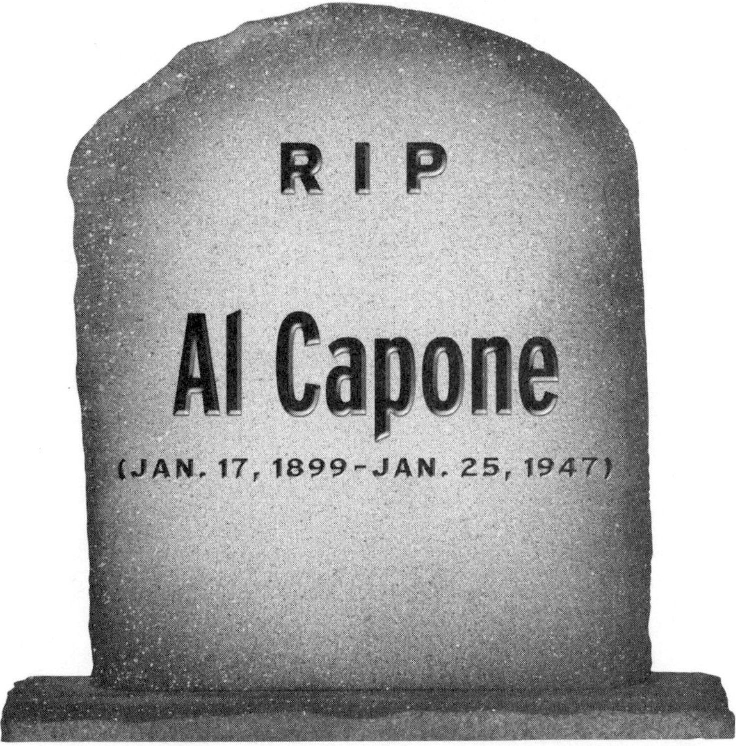
RIP
Al Capone
(JAN. 17, 1899–JAN. 25, 1947)

HOTEL METROPOLE
Chicago, Illinois
Endicott 5-2000

✓ 1. If someone disagrees with me, just step back. Take a deep breath. Then cave their head in with a baseball bat. See if that helps.

2. Don't have unprotected sex.!

✓ 3. Visit San Francisco at least once in my life. (I hear it's beautiful.)

Al Capone   27

HOTEL METROPOLE
Chicago, Illinois
Endicott 5-2000

✓4. Smash somebody's
  brains out with a baseball
  bat at least once a week.

  5. Get more baseball bats.

✓b. Pay taxes.

HOTEL METROPOLE
Chicago, Illinois
Endicott 5-2000

✓ 7. Have seven men massacred on Valentine's Day. No, ten. No, seven. Call it the "Valentine's Day Massacre." (Anybody who doesn't want to be massacred gets their head smashed in with a baseball bat.)

R I P

Wilt
Chamberlain

(AUG. 21, 1936–OCT. 12, 1999)

Los Angeles Lakers
Wilt Chamberlin

✓1. Have sex with a different woman every day for the next 30 years.

2. Try to grow emotionally with a different woman each day for the next 30 years.

✓3. Get haircut.

✓4. Score 100 points in one game each day with a different woman for the next 30 years.

RIP

Charlie Chaplin

(APRIL 16, 1889–DEC. 25, 1977)

— Keystone Studios —

✓ 1. Speak up! (It's okay to talk in private.)

2. Ask Buster Keaton if he's the one who keeps calling but doesn't say anything.

— Keystone Studios —

✓ 3. Practice walking "regular."

✓ 4. Hire clown for kid's birthday party.

idea for movie: a parody of the Third Reich? —Funny stuff...

RIP

Marie Curie

(NOV. 7, 1867 – JULY 4, 1934)

My to-do list:

1. Ask the doctor why everything I touch melts.

✓ 2. Tell Pierre to stop using my elbow for nightlight.

3. Don't touch that stuff!

✓ 4. Pick up Nobel Prize.

Time for a career change? I hear they're hiring at the coal mines... maybe teaching's not too bad...

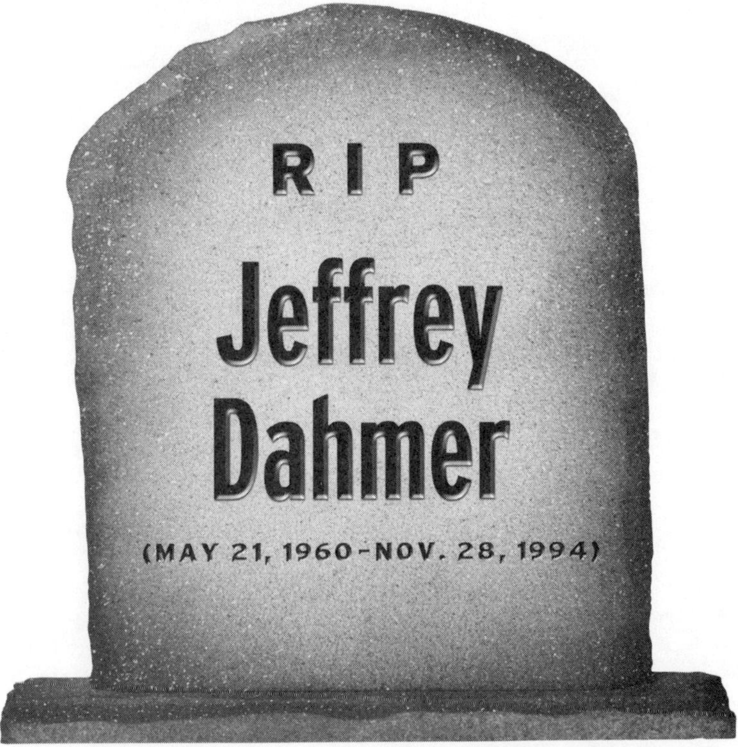
RIP
Jeffrey
Dahmer
(MAY 21, 1960–NOV. 28, 1994)

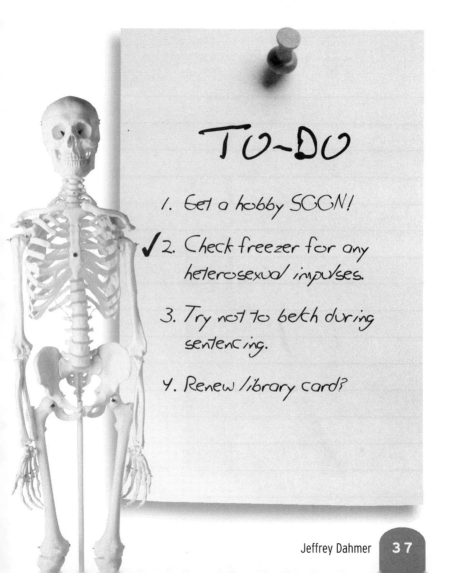

TO-DO

1. Get a hobby SOON!

✓ 2. Check freezer for any heterosexual impulses.

3. Try not to belch during sentencing.

4. Renew library card?

RIP

Charles Darwin

(FEB. 2, 1809–APRIL 26, 1882)

✺ To-Do List ✺

1. Legalize gambling on the Galápagos Islands?

2. Fifty push-ups a day, starting tomorrow. (Survival of the most fit!)

3. Twenty-five push-ups a day.

※ To-Do List ※

✔ 4. One push-up a day.
   But EVERY day!

✔ 5. Stop using the phrase
   "Well I'll be a monkey's
   uncle." (I lose credibility.)

Fitness centers? Why not?

RIP

Sammy
Davis Jr.

(DEC. 8, 1925–MAY 16, 1990)

Golden Nugget
·CASINO $ LAS VEGAS·

✓ 1. Clean eye.

✓ 2. Converted rice? (Maybe a tie-in or endorsement deal.)

✓ 3. Apologize to Frank every day. (Can't hurt.)

I'm 45 years old.
Time to drop the "junior."

RIP
Henry John
Deutschendorf Jr.
(aka John Denver)
(DEC. 31, 1943-OCT. 12, 1997)

❊ To-Do ❊

✓ 1. Drop the Henry!

✓ 2. Keep the Henry, lose the John?

✓ 3. Keep the John, keep the Henry, drop the Deutschendorf.

4. Don't "fill up my senses" before flying.

Henry John Deutschendorf Jr. (aka John Denver)

RIP

Emily
Dickinson

(DEC. 10, 1830–MAY 15, 1886)

Emily

✓ 1. *Spend some time alone.*

2. *Why must it rhyme...
Brother can you break a
twenty?*

3. *Have a big party and invite
all my friends.*

RIP

Joe DiMaggio

(NOV. 25, 1914–MARCH 8, 1999)

1. Look into endorsement deal for Tetley Tea. (Mr. "Tea"? I like it!)

✓2. Ask Marilyn "What's in it for you?"

3. Hide all of Marilyn's clothes.

NEW YORK YANKEES

NEW YORK, NEW YORK

✓ 4. Make another threatening call to Pete Rose. (Streak my ass, I've had marriages that lasted longer!)

5. Look up "joltin'."

Ask Marilyn to cook dinner (as an experiment).

WALT
DISNEY

✓ 1. Disney on ice? Just an idea.

2. Create a T.V. show: <u>The Wonderful World of Me.</u>

A mouse that talks, or maybe a duck with a speech impediment.... Whatever it is, it has to be something really goofy.

RIP

Amelia Earhart

(JULY 24, 1897–JULY 2, 1937)

TO-DO LIST:

✓ 1. Become first woman to fly across the Atlantic.

✓ 2. Become first woman to fly across the Pacific.

TO-DO LIST:

3. Double check Noonan's navigator creden-
tials. (Seems a bit sketchy, especially
about the flying stuff.)

4. Is the train so bad? Look into it.

RIP

Thomas Alva Edison

(FEB. 11, 1847 – OCT. 18, 1931)

THOMAS EDISON

✓ 1. Invent light bulb.

✓ 2. Patent it.

✓ 3. Invent motion picture projector.

✓ 4. Patent it.

5. Patent leather shoes.

6. Invent new middle name.

RIP

Albert Einstein

(MARCH 14, 1879–APRIL 18, 1955)

To-Do

1. E=MC and then some.

2. E=MC or something like that. . . .

3. The love you take is equal to the love you make.

4. BORING!

5. i'm starved.

TO-DO

6. Bring on the chicks!

7. Try a large tube of Bryllcreem.

8. Spend more time—some time—with the kids.

Things equal to "E" are equal to themselves. Everything is equal to itself.

RIP

Dwight D. Eisenhower

(OCT. 14, 1890-MARCH 28, 1969)

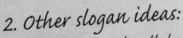

✪ Dwight D. Eisenhower
United States Army ✪

✓1. Rework "I'm fond of Ike" campaign slogan.

2. Other slogan ideas:
   – Dwight is right all day and all night.
   – If you're looking for power: Eisenhower.
   – Vote for me: My name is Eisenhower.

RIP

F. Scott Fitzgerald

(SEP. 24, 1896–DEC. 21, 1940)

F. SCOTT FITZGERALD

1. Tell everybody the "F" also stands for "Fitzgerald."

2. Write the definitive American novel, <u>The Great Gatsby</u>... but in comic book form.

3. Commit Zelda...but wait till after the party.

RIP

Jim Fixx

(APRIL 13, 1932–JULY 20, 1984)

Dr. James Fixx

✓ 1. Run to store.

✓ 2. Run to work.

✓ 3. Run downstairs
   and get the laundry.

✓ 4. Run upstairs.

✓ 5. Write a book about running and tell everyone how good it is for you.

6. Don't drop dead from too much running, you know what they say....

RIP

Henry Ford

(JULY 30, 1863 – APRIL 7, 1947)

Ford Motor Company
Detroit, Michigan

✓ 1. Revolutionize America with assembly line method.

2. Work on company slogan: "Have you driven a car yet?" or "Look, it's a car not a horse."

3. Call new car . . . the Ford Pinto?

✓ 4. Call new car . . . the Model "T" (better!)

RIP

Benjamin Franklin

(JAN. 17, 1706–APRIL 17, 1790)

Benjamin Franklin

✓ 1. Don't pose for anything less than the $100 bill.

✓ 2. Buy a kite. (If anyone asks, say it's for an experiment.)

Benjamin Franklin

✓ 3. Invent a place from which you can borrow books.

4. Call "The Place from Which You Can Borrow Books."

"early to bed, early to rise, makes old Ben a very sleepy guy"... "early to bed, early to rise, makes a man healthy, wealthy, and ... shit!"... "early to bed, early to rise, makes... for a long day!"

RIP

Sigmund Freud

(MAY 6, 1856 – SEP. 23, 1939)

R̟x̟   Dr. Sigmund Freud

1. Try to talk about infantile
   sexuality in a way that
   doesn't alienate the kids.

✓ 2. Dream on.

Rethink the whole "penis envy" thing ...
I must've been high or something.
On the other hand, who's gonna check?

Physician's Signature

Dispense as written   Refill ___ times

RIP

Robert Frost

(MARCH 26, 1874–JAN. 29, 1963)

Things To-Do Today

1. Is it cold in here or is it just my name? (Great pick-up line! Try it.)

Work in progress: Two roads diverged in a yellow wood — what are the odds? — I took the one less traveled (with the exception of me) because why? — Needs work.

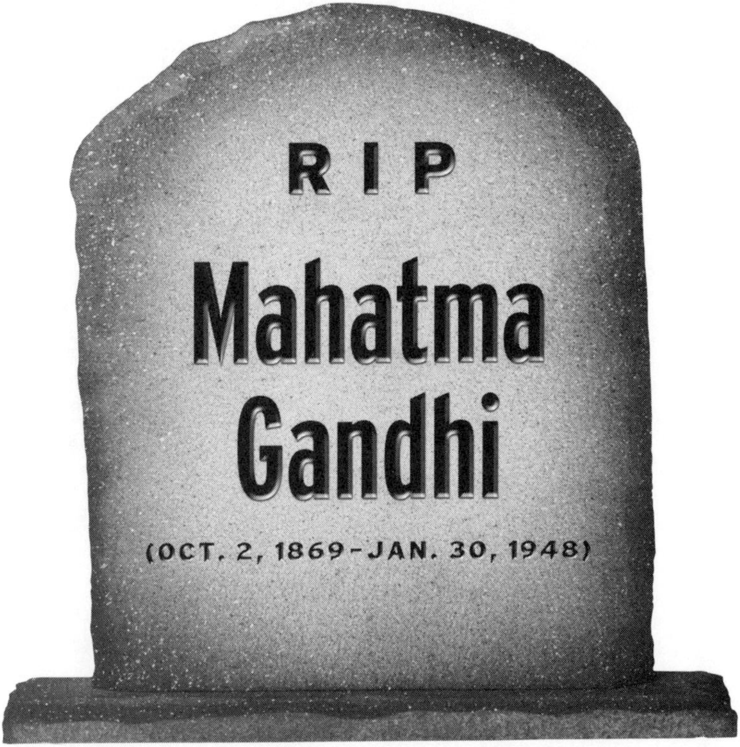
RIP
Mahatma
Gandhi
(OCT. 2, 1869–JAN. 30, 1948)

To-Do List —

1. A shake for breakfast, a shake for lunch, and a sensible dinner.

2. Get a fun-house mirror, I'll look even skinnier!

3. Clip coupons.

✓ 4. Find better way to make point because I am VERY, VERY HUNGRY!

RIP

Jerry Garcia

(AUG. 1, 1942–AUG. 9, 1995)

To-Do:

1. Hire an arranger.

2. Do something other than drugs.

3. Eat right.

4. Take dog for walk.

5. Call plumber.

6. Find out tour dates.
   (is it today?)

TO-DO:

7. Hire a maid.

8. Take tie to dry cleaners. (Those wild, colorful stains aren't coming out)

9. Change name of group from "Grateful Dead" to "Glad to be Comatose."

RIP

Judy Garland

(JUNE 10, 1922-JUNE 22, 1969)

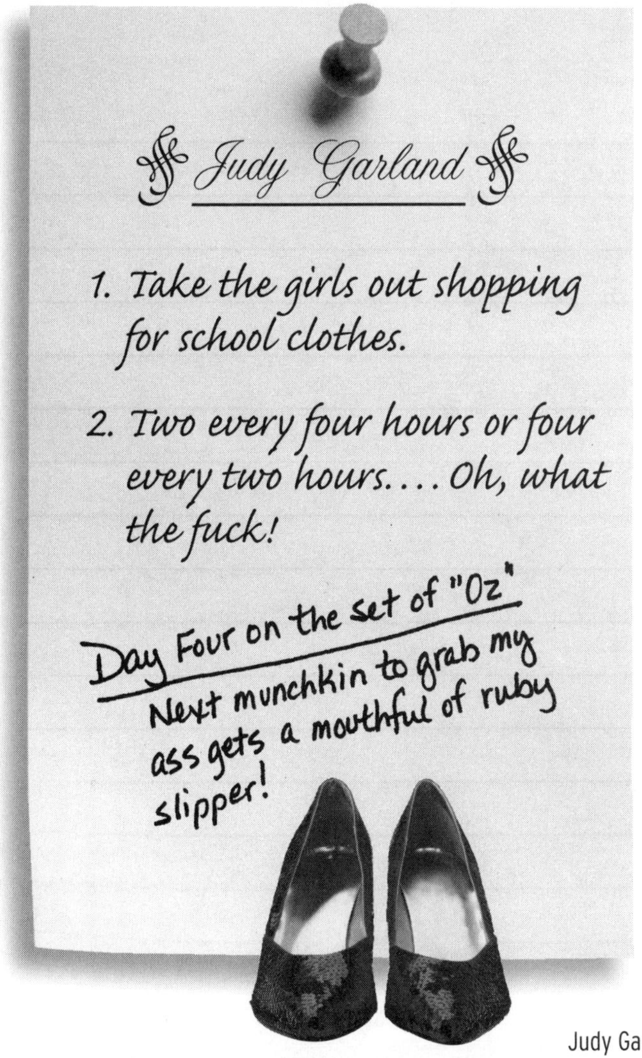
Judy Garland
1. Take the girls out shopping for school clothes.
2. Two every four hours or four every two hours. . . . Oh, what the fuck!
Day Four on the set of "Oz"
Next munchkin to grab my ass gets a mouthful of ruby slipper!

RIP

Lou Gehrig
(JUNE 19, 1903–JUNE 2, 1941)

NEW YORK YANKEES

1. Call in sick.

2. Get a candy bar named after me.

✓ 3. Get a disease named after me.
   (Though I'd prefer the candy bar.)

4. Work on retirement speech:
   "I consider myself the luckiest man on the face of the earth ... with the possible exception of Joe Piscopo."

Babe eats 10 hot dogs– before noon, drinks 20 beers a day and stays out all night with hookers, and I'm the one who gets the deadly disease. ... Ain't that a kick in the head!

Lou Gehrig

RIP
Theodor
Seuss Geisel
(aka Dr. Seuss)
(MARCH 2, 1904–SEP. 24, 1991)

Things to do:

1. Find something that rhymes with Geisel.

2. Erotic poetry doesn't seem to be working out, but the kids seem to like it.

✓ 3. Take eggs back to store; they look green.

RIP
Ulysses S. Grant
(APR. 27, 1822–JULY 23, 1885)

COMMANDER IN CHIEF
★ UNION ARMY ★

✓ 1. Ask Mom what the "S" stands for.

2. Lead Union forces to victory over the ~~East~~ South.

3. Find out who's buried in my tomb.

COMMANDER IN CHIEF
★ UNION ARMY ★

4. Lincoln Schmincoln.
   No one's shooting at him

✓ 5. Meet Robert E. Lee for the signing of
   the surrender, but don't make it any harder
   than it already is.

6. Ask Lee what the "E" stands for.

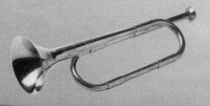

RIP

Lorne Greene

(FEB. 12, 1915–SEP. 11, 1987)

THINGS TO DO:

✓1. Try to put words to theme music—dum didda dum didda dum didda dum Bonanza, dum didda dum didda dum didda dum dum didda we're cowboys. (Repeat.)

2. Ask Michael Landon if he knows why show is called <u>Bonanza</u>.

THINGS TO DO:

3. Ask Dan Blocker if he knows why show is called <u>Bonanza</u>—somebody's gotta know!

Ask the producers why my eldest son is older than me. And why is the show called <u>Bonanza</u>???

RIP

Gus Grissom

(APR. 3, 1926–JAN. 27, 1967)

Gus Grissom—NASA

1. Bring extra socks just in case.

2. Explain one more time to wife that "you can get killed crossing the street," but in a way that is not so menacing. (After a while it starts to sound like a suggestion.)

Gus Grissom—NASA

3. Try the freeze-dried veal.

4. Bring a six-pack.

Why do they bother with these mission simulations anyway; they're such a waste of time.

RIP

John Hancock

(JAN. 12, 1737–OCT. 8, 1793)

To-Do:

1. Tell Jefferson the Declaration of Independence is good, very good, but he might want to trim it just a tad.

2. Get drunk with Sam Adams.

3. Fly a kite with Ben Franklin.

4. Get new friends.

We the People *of the United States, in o...*

To-Do:

✓ 5. Sign the Declaration of Independence. (But _really_ sign it!)

6. Tell Jefferson that it's important that I'm the first to sign this thing, because, because ... come up with a reason later.

That's right... Hancock!

J. H.

Johnny "The Hand" Hancock

Hancock ... John Hancock

Johnny H.

To-Do List:

1. Outlive Janis Joplin.
✓ 2. Get high.
✓ 3. Hang out in San Francisco.
✓ 4. Try playing the guitar lefty.

RIP
Henry the VIII
(JUNE 28, 1491–JAN. 28, 1547)

FROM THE COURT OF
HENRY VIII

✓ 1. Tell Anne that lately she's been getting on my nerves.

✓ 2. Tell Catherine that lately she's been getting on my nerves.

FROM THE COURT OF
HENRY VIII

✓ 3. Tell Sir Thomas Moore that lately he's been getting on my nerves.

RIP

Patrick
Henry

(MAY 29, 1736–JUNE 6, 1799)

To-Do:

1. Try not to just blurt things out!

RIP

Jim Henson

(SEP. 24, 1936–MAY 16, 1990)

Things to do:

1. Spend more time with people.

2. Try talking without the socks on my hands.

3. Work on a T.V. show concept starring a frog and a pig and a homeless drunkard called Mr. Pisso.

RIP

Adolf Hitler

(APRIL 20, 1889–APRIL 30, 1945)

✠ ADOLF HITLER ✠

1. Don't give up on painting.
   (It's what keeps me sane!)

2. Do something with
   my hair.

✠ ADOLF HITLER ✠

3. Get something special for Eva. (Maybe earrings or a nice fragrance or maybe a big Slavic nation.)

When speaking publicly: Always stand up straight, try to make eye contact with as many people as possible, and <u>scream</u>!

RIP

Buddy Holly

(SEP. 7, 1936–FEB. 3, 1959)

BUDDY

1. Never fly with anyone named "The Big Bopper."

RIP

Joan of Arc

(C. 1412–MAY 30, 1431)

Things to do—

✓ 1. Lead France to victory before I'm fifteen.

2. Find out if Jean Luc likes me or if he "likes me" likes me.

3. Pick up a flame-retardant ensemble.

Ask God what's in it for me.

RIP

Janis Joplin

(JAN. 19, 1943–OCT. 4, 1970)

✎ TO-DO LIST: ✎

✓ 1. Outlive Jimi Hendrix.

✓ 2. Get high.

✓ 3. Hang out in San Francisco.

RIP

Jack Kerouac

(MARCH 12, 1922-OCT. 21, 1969)

» Things to do — «

1. Find self.

2. Lose Ginsberg.

3. Find Ginsberg.

4. Lose self.

» Things to do — «

✓ 5. Influence a generation.

6. Get a good map.

✓ 7. Experiment with drugs.

8. If someone insults me in a barroom just ignore them.

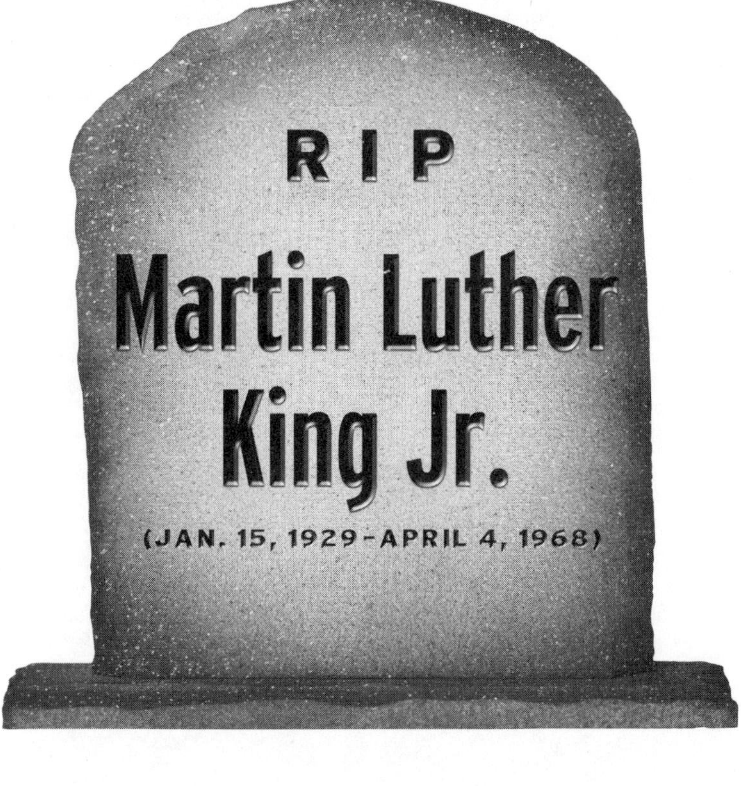
RIP
Martin Luther King Jr.
(JAN. 15, 1929–APRIL 4, 1968)

m.L.K., Jr.

✓ 1. Talk about the dream again, but this time really "sell it."

2. Don't get shot. (Lotta nuts out there!)

✓ 3. Lead civil rights march on Washington, D.C., but if the police ask, we're on a tour.

RIP

Timothy Leary

(OCT. 22, 1920–MAY 31, 1996)

To-Do List

✓ 1. Tell my dad to stop melting.

✓ 2. Tune in, turn on, and drop by once in a while. . . . (Work in progress.)

3. Expand consciousness. Start with a new suit!

To-Do List

✓ 4. Drop acid.

5. Pick up acid. (Stop dropping it.)

Note to self:
Hey, I'm talking
to myself... this
is good acid...

John

1. Find a hobby for Yoko or I'll kill one of us.

✓ 2. Tell her she can't join the Beatles. We're full.

3. Tell her if she wants to pose nude that's her business.

RIP

John Lennon

(OCT. 9, 1940–DEC. 8, 1980)

4. Tell her that after her singing the sound of fingernails on a chalkboard is soothing.

5. Beatles reunion?

✓ 6. Write a new song about peace, love and brotherhood.

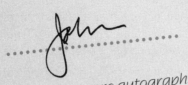

7. Don't sign any more autographs.
   (There are some real weirdos
   out there.)

8. Return Pete Best's call!

Idea for a song — "Imagine there's
no Beatles... but still royalties..."
"I don't believe in Beatles, I just believe
in me. Yoko and me, and I'm not
really sure about Yoko..."

R I P

(MAY 16, 1919-FEB. 4, 1987)

Liberace

✓ 1. Assure my public that I'm not gay.

2. Hire four new houseboys.

3. Fire four old houseboys.

4. Nah, keep all the houseboys!

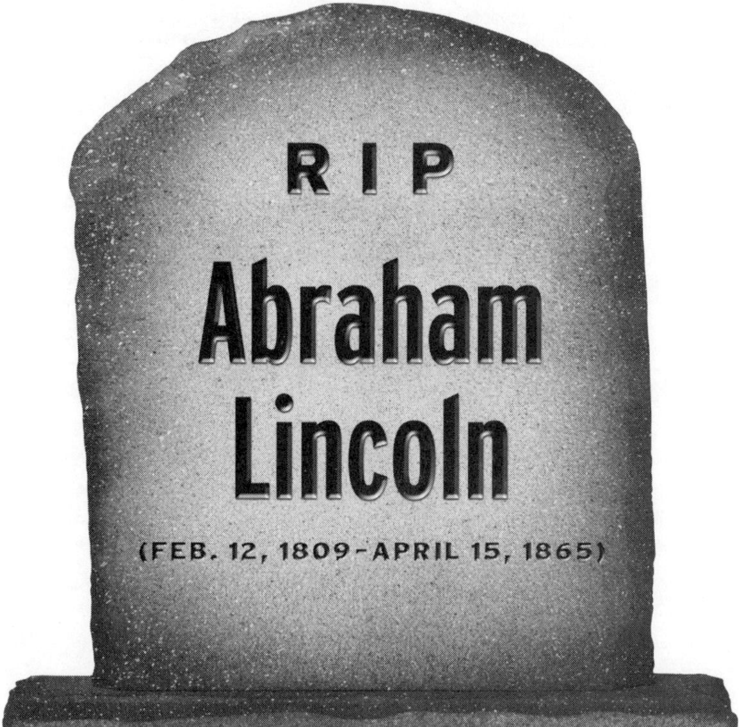
RIP
Abraham Lincoln
(FEB. 12, 1809-APRIL 15, 1865)

Abraham Lincoln

THE WHITE HOUSE
WASHINGTON

✓ 1. Free slaves.

✓ 2. Think of fancy way to say "eighty-seven years ago."

3. Beef up security at Ford's Theatre.

The South must not prevail!!
But God, I love those grits!

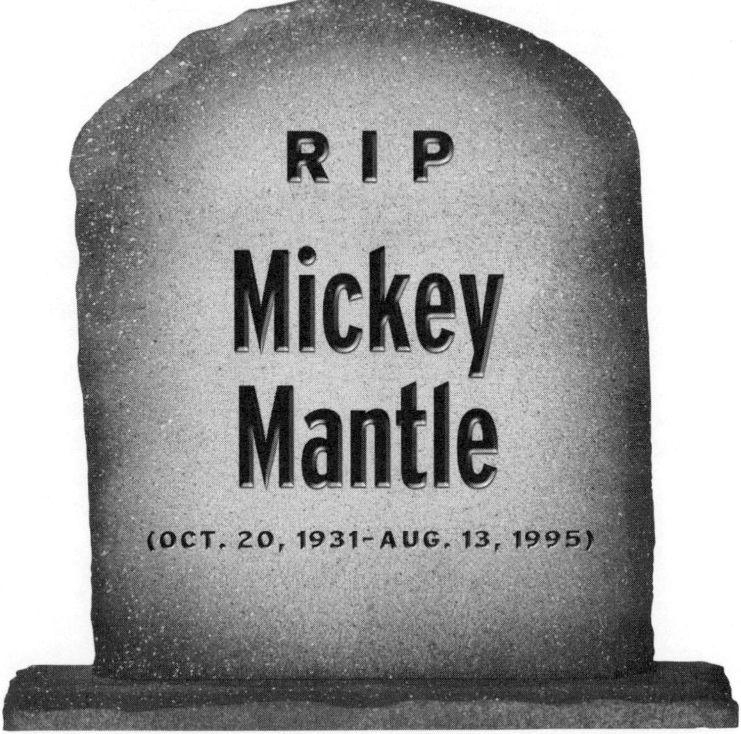
RIP
Mickey
Mantle
(OCT. 20, 1931-AUG. 13, 1995)

NEW YORK YANKEES

NEW YORK, NEW YORK

✓ 1. When I tell people I'm a "switch-hitter," they laugh. Look into this.

2. What about the idea of a "Mickey" mantle? A place to keep your trophies. Possibility.

Who's this other "Mickey" everyone's talking about?

Mickey Mantle   119

RIP
Senator
Joseph
McCarthy
(NOV. 14, 1908–MAY 2, 1957)

Joseph McCarthy
Senate Committee on UnAmerican Activities

1. How well do I know _myself_ ?

2. Make sure no one sees me
   bringing my dry cleaning to
   Linsky's. (If someone does see
   me, just tell them I'm getting
   my pants cleaned.)

Joseph McCarthy
Senate Committee on UnAmerican Activities

3. How well do I know Linsky?

4. How well do I know my pants?

Check out this actor guy, Red Buttons ...
he's gotta be a Communist. I mean, it's
in his name for Pete's sake. "RED."
People, come on!

RIP

William McKinley

(JAN. 29, 1843–SEP. 14, 1901)

1. Don't forget to come up with a catchy phrase for remembering the Maine Battleship.

2. See if Spain will take Rhode island for Guam.

RIP

Marilyn Monroe

(JUNE 1, 1926 – AUG. 5, 1962)

Things to do:

✓1. Pout.

✓2. Call JFK. (If Jackie answers, hang up!)

✓3. Marry Joe D. (I'm not sure what he does, but I heard he has a nice stroke.)

4. Finish all the old pills before I start the new ones.

Marilyn Monroe 125

RIP

Elizabeth
Montgomery

(APRIL 15, 1933–MAY 18, 1995)

Columbia Pictures

✓ 1. Try and turn this nervous nose twitch into a strength.

✓ 2. Do a TV movie about a woman that gets raped, rescued, and then raped again. Maybe one more rape ... over credits?

3. Dick York, Dick Sargent, any Dick will do, just get me a new Darrin!

Elizabeth Montgomery

RIP

Jim Morrison

(DEC. 8, 1943–JULY 3, 1971)

🎵 To-Do 🎵

✓1. Get a rhyming dictionary.

✓2. "I AM THE AMPHIBIAN KING" (Needs work.)

3. Chew vomit slowly.

RIP

Benito
Mussolini

(JULY 29, 1883–APRIL 28, 1945)

Things to do

✓ 1. When we choose sides pick the German guy.
   (Or at least don't get on his bad side.)

RIP

Richard Nixon

(JAN. 9, 1913–APRIL 22, 1994)

Richard M. Nixon

THE WHITE HOUSE
WASHINGTON

✓ 1. Screw the country.

✓ 2. Deny everything.

✓ 3. Cancel subscription to the Washington Post.

✓ 4. *Record every conversation.*
  (You never know when this
  might come in handy.)

G. Gordon Liddy?
I thought everyone was saying,
"Gee, Gordon Liddy."

RIP

Noah

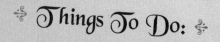

❖ Things To Do: ❖

✓1. Build ark.

2. No shirt, no shoes, no service.

3. Build something nice for the wife, too. (Window box? Or maybe an ashtray.)

❧ Things To Do: ❧

4. ABSOLUTELY NO PETS!
   (Insurance issue.)

Don't be afraid to ask God
to repeat himself... this stuff is
important!

RIP

Nostradamus

(DEC. 14, 1503–JULY 2, 1566)

ΠOSTRADAMUS

1. Tell my literary agent not to worry about the predictions, just worry about closing the deal.

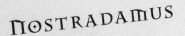

NOSTRADAMUS

✓2. Make sure the predictions are catastrophic and WELL into the future. (Good luck proving me wrong!)

3. Y2K?

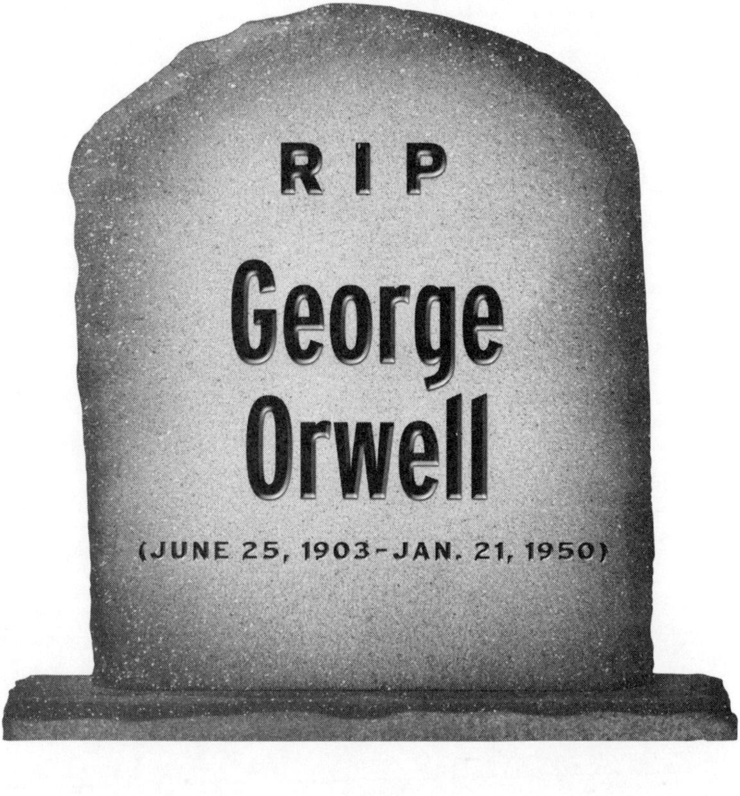
RIP
George
Orwell
(JUNE 25, 1903-JAN. 21, 1950)

To-Do

1. "1984" might be too specific. (Change title to "1973," my lucky numbers.)

2. Write a terrifying book about society being under the constant surveillance of . . . BIG GRANDMOTHER!!!

3. Forget the condemnation of a totalitarian society. Lighten up. Write a joke.

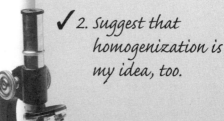

RIP

Louis Pasteur

(DEC. 27, 1822–SEP. 28, 1895)

※ **To-Do List:** ※

✓ 1. Try to negotiate strong deal on the whole "pasteurization" thing.

✓ 2. Suggest that homogenization is my idea, too.

✳ To-Do List: ✳

✓ 3. Look into this rabies thing ... could be big bucks.

4. Thank the silk industry for the nice scarves, but I don't need anymore!

RIP

Pablo Picasso

(OCT. 25, 1881–APRIL 8, 1973)

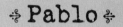

÷ Pablo ÷

1. Check eyes for a stronger prescription.

✓2. Blue period.

✓3. Rose period.

✦ Pablo ✦

4. Paisley period.

5. Punch the next person who asks if I'm "on drugs."

RIP

James Polk

(NOV. 2, 1795 – JUNE 15, 1849)

JAMES POLK

THE WHITE HOUSE
WASHINGTON

1. Leave legacy.

✓ 2. Leave.

3. Make sure they remember me as the guy between Tyler and...who did I lose to?

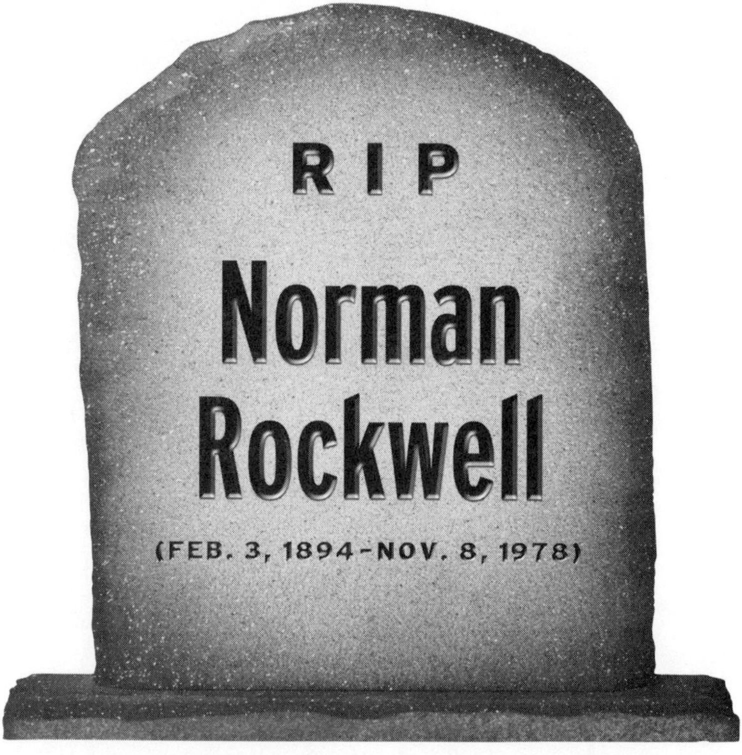
RIP
Norman Rockwell
(FEB. 3, 1894–NOV. 8, 1978)

To-Do List —

✓1. Tell kids it's for art.

✓2. See if "Americana" is copyrighted.

3. Submit painting of severed head to <u>Saturday Evening Post</u> (Just to see their reaction).

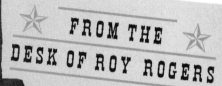

RIP

Roy Rogers

(NOV. 5, 1911–JULY 6, 1998)

FROM THE
DESK OF ROY ROGERS

✓ 1. Horse meat with all the fixin's. Yeah!

✓ 2. Trigger is the horse,
Dale is the wife—
REMEMBER THIS!

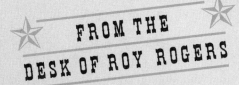

FROM THE
DESK OF ROY ROGERS

3. Challenge Gene Autry to a
   singing showdown.

4. Start a chain of fancy restaurants.
   (But keep them off the highways.)

RIP

Will Rogers

(NOV. 4, 1879 – AUG. 15, 1935)

✪ Things to Do: ✪

✓1. Come up with catchy phrase
people will remember like:

"I never met a guy quite
like you" or "Hot enough
for ya?"

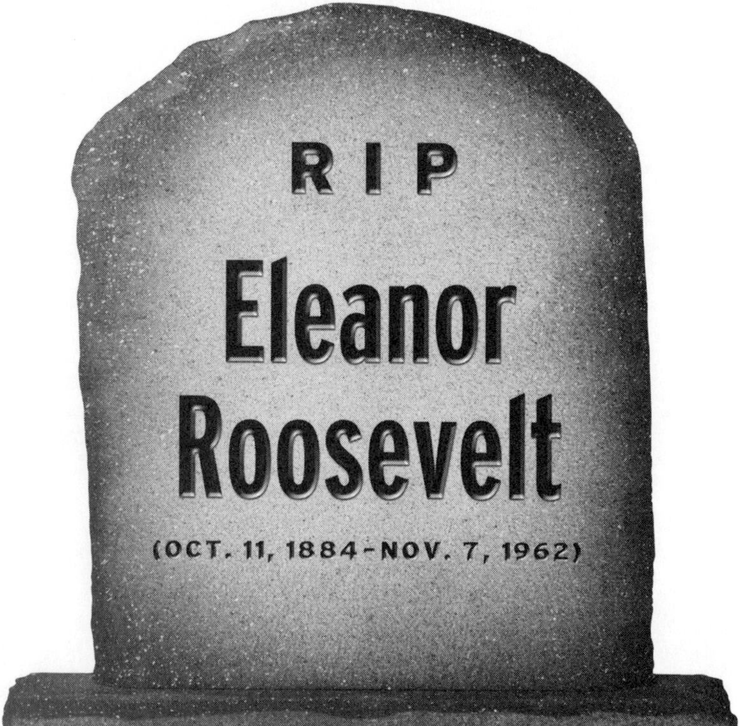
RIP
Eleanor
Roosevelt
(OCT. 11, 1884-NOV. 7, 1962)

First Lady Eleanor Roosevelt
The White House   Washington

✓ 1. Get a makeover.

2. Get a TOTAL makeover.
   (Last one didn't take.)

3. Don't let Franklin
   push me around
   just because....

RIP

Franklin D. Roosevelt

(JAN. 30, 1882–APR. 12, 1945)

President Franklin D. Roosevelt
White House
Washington

✓ 1. Think of at least one more thing we have to fear (for speech): dwarfs, the dark, the color blue, musicals (why are they singing?)

President Franklin D. Roosevelt

Washington

The White House

2. Come up with another name for
   the Great Depression.
   Something more upbeat, like
   the "Pretty Bad Depression"
   or "It Could Be Worse," or
   "Let's Hope It Doesn't
   Get Worse."

✓3. Wear pants that breathe.
   (For fireside chats.)

Things to do today:

✓1. *Say something nice about Roger.*

2. *Work on joke about opposable thumbs.*

✓3. *Rent The Godfather — my credibility's at stake here.*

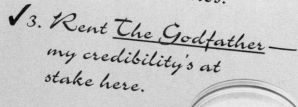

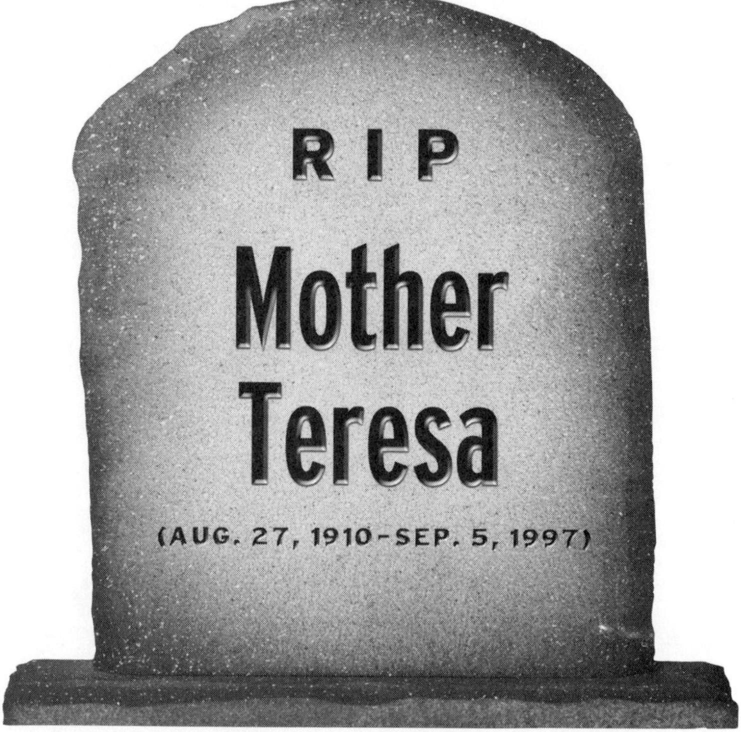
RIP
Mother
Teresa
(AUG. 27, 1910–SEP. 5, 1997)

To-Do:

✓ 1. Return calls to Pope.
   (I need voice mail!)

2. Perform a miracle. (Soon.)

Get tickets to see that show,
<u>OCalcutta.</u> A charming evening at
the theater would be a welcome
break from all the poverty that
I deal with on a daily basis.

RIP

Karl
Wallenda

(C. 1905–MARCH 22, 1978)

Things To Do:

✓1. Take the family out for a walk across the high wire.

2. Get a big net, so I don't fall to my fucking death.

3. Don't do anything T.O.O. stupid; it may result in me falling to my fucking death.

What about just "walking a fine line"?

To-Do List:

1. Get some sun.

2. Don't be such a "gloomy Gus"!

✓3. Paint a picture of a Campbell's Soup can. (Could it really be that simple?)

4. Everybody has seventeen minutes of fame. (Too much?)

5. How about fifteen minutes of <u>sun</u>?

6. Twenty minutes of free local calls?

RIP

George Washington

(FEB. 22, 1732–DEC. 14, 1799)

George Washington
Mount Vernon, Virginia

✓ 1. Cross Delaware. (But tell Martha I just went out for some air.)

✓ 2. Check gums for termites.

3. Bury the hatchet.

4. Drop the "Father of Our Country" thing—makes Martha uncomfortable.

RIP

Orson Welles

(MAY 6, 1915–OCT. 10, 1985)

ORSON WELLES

✓ 1. Scare the shit out of the whole fucking world.

✓ 2. Write, direct, and star in a motion picture that will have cinematic ramifications for years to come.

✓ 3. Do wine commercials on TV and scare the shit out of the whole fucking world at the sight of my enormous girth.

RIP

Tammy Wynette

(MAY 5, 1942 – APRIL 6, 1998)

✪ Things to do ✪

✓ 1. Rework "stand near your van" song (has possibilities).

✓ 2. Do whatever my man says.

3. Clean trailer.

4. Try not to be in a stormy relationship.

About the Author

Jonathan Katz is an accomplished stand-up comic, musician, actor, and writer. Katz cocreated, writes, and stars in the hit animated series *Dr. Katz: Professional Therapist,* which airs on Comedy Central and has been heralded by both *Time* magazine and *TV Guide* as one of the ten best shows on television. For his work on the series, Katz has received an Emmy Award for Outstanding Prime-Time Voiceover Performance (marking the first-ever Emmy for Comedy Central), the prestigious Peabody Award for Excellence in Broadcasting, and two Cable Ace Awards for Best Animation, Special or Series, and for Best Short-Form Programming.

His additional television credits include: his own HBO special, a recurring role on CBS's *Ink,* a recurring role as himself in the final season of HBO's *The Larry Sanders Show,* and numerous guest appearances on *The Late Show with David Letterman, The Tonight Show,* and *Politically Incorrect with Bill Maher,* for which he also served as creative consultant.

In the feature film arena, he cowrote the story for the critically acclaimed film *House of Games* with David Mamet. He has appeared in two additional Mamet films, *Spanish Prisoner* and *Things Change,* and has roles in the upcoming films *The Independent,* which stars Janeane Garofalo, and Mamet's newest film, *State and Main,* with Alec Baldwin and Sarah Jessica Parker. Additionally, Katz has feature film projects at DreamWorks and FOX 2000.

Originally a musician and songwriter, Katz fronted a rhythm and blues group called Katz and Jammers before serving as the musical director for Robin Williams's 1979 stand-up tour. In 1981 he started working solo, doing a mostly musical cabaret act. In between songs he began to lay the groundwork for his stand-up act.

A native New Yorker, Jonathan moved to Boston fourteen years ago and currently resides in Newton, Massachusetts, with his wife and two daughters.